JOURNAL FOR THE CULTURAL TRAVELER

A TRAVELER'S JOURNAL

Commonwealth Editions
an imprint of Applewood Books
Carlisle, Massachusetts

For a custom edition of A Traveler's Journal
with an image from your institution, site, or collection,
please contact customercare@awb.com.

Cover image: "See America, Visit the National Parks,"
created by Harry Herzog for the WPA, 1940.

978-1-5162-6025-6

Published by Commonwealth Editions
an imprint of Applewood Books
Carlisle, Massachusetts 01741
www.commonwealtheditions.com

To inquire about this edition
or to request a free copy
of our current catalog
featuring our best-selling books, write to:
Applewood Books
P.O. Box 27
Carlisle, MA 01741
For more complete listings,
visit us on the web at:
www.awb.com

Manufactured in the United States of America

YOUR MOST PERSONAL SOUVENIR

"These empty pages are your future,
soon to become your past.
They will read the most personal tale
you shall ever find in a book."
—ANONYMOUS

The most personal travel keepsake you could ever own is right in your hands. However, just owning this book is not enough; you need to really use it. And once you do it for one trip, you will want a journal for all of your travels, recording the essence of why you ventured out, how your journey progressed, and the personal memories you might have forgotten if they were not captured within these pages.

Keeping a travel journal is a deeply personal pursuit. Write whatever you think you'll want to remember twenty years from now and won't be able to find in a generic guidebook or on a website. That can include the places you stay, the people you encounter, things you find funny, and the sensory memories—smells, sounds, tastes, etc.—that make your trip unique to you. Write about any major milestones or personal discoveries, and always include the disasters and misadventures—these will make the best stories to share with others for years to come. The writing prompts at the beginning of each section can help spark ideas of what to write. Be sure to circle the month and day at the top of each page to help record your time line.

Throughout this book you will find pages that are blank except for a travel quote from some distinguished journal keepers. These pages are intended to give you the space to draw an object, scene, or feeling you want to remember but can't capture well in a photo. You can also use this space to add items to your book, such as tickets, postcards, menus, etc.

In order to keep all of your information in one place, you will find pages in the back of the book that provide space for packing lists provide helpful travel tips and conversion tables. There is also a "point page" for those times you find yourself in a place where you do not speak the language but need to communicate and can do so best through universal symbols. Be sure to put your contact information in the back, so if by chance the book is lost, a friendly passerby can return it to you.

Every journal entry doesn't have to be brilliant—just try to write at least something every day. Writing even small details each day will help you maintain your momentum. Sometimes if you miss writing for even a couple of days, those days can quickly become the entire trip—so try to write something, no matter how small.

"People who keep journals have life twice."
—Jessamyn West

A TRAVELER'S JOURNAL

(Destination)

(Dates)

GREEN
LAND
USA
USA

PREPARE

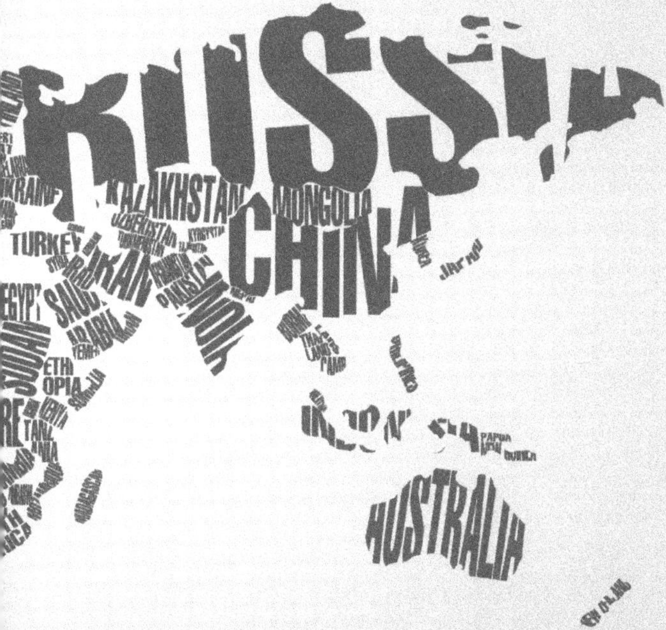

"I haven't been everywhere, but it's on my list."
—Susan Sontag

Choices, preparation, anticipation

How did you decide on this destination?

What are some things you are anticipating about this trip?

What excites you the most?

What makes you nervous?

What do you think the place will be like?

What are things you want to see or activities you want to do?

Is there anything you hope to accomplish on this trip?

Any goals you set for yourself?

Did you buy anything new especially for this trip?

What is one thing you brought that you should have left at home?

JAN FEB MAR APR MAY JUN JUL AUG SEP OCT NOV DEC

1 2 3 4 5 6 7 8 9 10 11 12 13 14 15 16 17 18 19 20 21 22 23 24 25 26 27 28 29 30 31

JAN FEB MAR APR MAY JUN JUL AUG SEP OCT NOV DEC

1 2 3 4 5 6 7 8 9 10 11 12 13 14 15 16 17 18 19 20 21 22 23 24 25 26 27 28 29 30 31

JAN FEB MAR APR MAY JUN JUL AUG SEP OCT NOV DEC

1 2 3 4 5 6 7 8 9 10 11 12 13 14 15 16 17 18 19 20 21 22 23 24 25 26 27 28 29 30 31

BON VOYAGE

"Keep a notebook.
Travel with it, eat with it, sleep with it.
Slap into it every stray thought that flutters up into your brain.
Cheap paper is less perishable than gray matter,
and lead pencil markings endure longer than memory."

—Jack London

Travel companions, travel habits, troubleshooting

Who is traveling with you?

What are three things your travel companion should know about you?

Have them write down three things they think you should know about them.

What modes of transportation will you use to get to your destination?

Write about your habits and things you like to bring on a bus/plane/train/car trip.

Did you run into any problems on your journey?

How did you fix them?

Did anything positive come out of this, like meeting someone nice because of an unexpected delay?

JAN FEB MAR APR MAY JUN JUL AUG SEP OCT NOV DEC

1 2 3 4 5 6 7 8 9 10 11 12 13 14 15 16 17 18 19 20 21 22 23 24 25 26 27 28 29 30 31

JAN FEB MAR APR MAY JUN JUL AUG SEP OCT NOV DEC

1 2 3 4 5 6 7 8 9 10 11 12 13 14 15 16 17 18 19 20 21 22 23 24 25 26 27 28 29 30 31

"I have found out there ain't no surer way to find out whether you like people or hate them than to travel with them."

—Mark Twain

JAN FEB MAR APR MAY JUN JUL AUG SEP OCT NOV DEC

1 2 3 4 5 6 7 8 9 10 11 12 13 14 15 16 17 18 19 20 21 22 23 24 25 26 27 28 29 30 31

JAN FEB MAR APR MAY JUN JUL AUG SEP OCT NOV DEC

1 2 3 4 5 6 7 8 9 10 11 12 13 14 15 16 17 18 19 20 21 22 23 24 25 26 27 28 29 30 31

JAN FEB MAR APR MAY JUN JUL AUG SEP OCT NOV DEC

1 2 3 4 5 6 7 8 9 10 11 12 13 14 15 16 17 18 19 20 21 22 23 24 25 26 27 28 29 30 31

JAN FEB MAR APR MAY JUN JUL AUG SEP OCT NOV DEC

1 2 3 4 5 6 7 8 9 10 11 12 13 14 15 16 17 18 19 20 21 22 23 24 25 26 27 28 29 30 31

EXPLORE

"One's destination is never a place, but rather a new way of looking at things."

—Henry Miller

You have arrived…

Note the time and write a few sentences
about what you are doing.
Do this several times throughout the day.

Use your senses.
What can you see, smell, taste, hear, and feel?

Draw a picture of something you see, big or small.
What were the highlights of today? List five things.
Do this throughout your trip.

Write about someone you met today.
Recall their appearance, their personality and
mannerisms, the conversation you had with them.
How did they make you feel?

What surprised you the most today?

Look around and observe.
List all the things you see–interactions between
people, people at work or at leisure, your surroundings,
buildings and vehicles, animals and plants.

JAN FEB MAR APR MAY JUN JUL AUG SEP OCT NOV DEC

1 2 3 4 5 6 7 8 9 10 11 12 13 14 15 16 17 18 19 20 21 22 23 24 25 26 27 28 29 30 31

JAN FEB MAR APR MAY JUN JUL AUG SEP OCT NOV DEC

1 2 3 4 5 6 7 8 9 10 11 12 13 14 15 16 17 18 19 20 21 22 23 24 25 26 27 28 29 30 31

"Never go on trips with anyone you do not love."

—Ernest Hemingway

JAN FEB MAR APR MAY JUN JUL AUG SEP OCT NOV DEC

1 2 3 4 5 6 7 8 9 10 11 12 13 14 15 16 17 18 19 20 21 22 23 24 25 26 27 28 29 30 31

JAN FEB MAR APR MAY JUN JUL AUG SEP OCT NOV DEC

1 2 3 4 5 6 7 8 9 10 11 12 13 14 15 16 17 18 19 20 21 22 23 24 25 26 27 28 29 30 31

JAN FEB MAR APR MAY JUN JUL AUG SEP OCT NOV DEC

1 2 3 4 5 6 7 8 9 10 11 12 13 14 15 16 17 18 19 20 21 22 23 24 25 26 27 28 29 30 31

"Take time to look..."
—Georgia O'Keeffe

JAN FEB MAR APR MAY JUN JUL AUG SEP OCT NOV DEC

1 2 3 4 5 6 7 8 9 10 11 12 13 14 15 16 17 18 19 20 21 22 23 24 25 26 27 28 29 30 31

JAN FEB MAR APR MAY JUN JUL AUG SEP OCT NOV DEC

1 2 3 4 5 6 7 8 9 10 11 12 13 14 15 16 17 18 19 20 21 22 23 24 25 26 27 28 29 30 31

JAN FEB MAR APR MAY JUN JUL AUG SEP OCT NOV DEC

1 2 3 4 5 6 7 8 9 10 11 12 13 14 15 16 17 18 19 20 21 22 23 24 25 26 27 28 29 30 31

"Perhaps travel cannot prevent bigotry, but by demonstrating that all peoples cry, laugh, eat, worry, and die, it can introduce the idea that if we try and understand each other, we may even become friends."

—Maya Angelou

JAN FEB MAR APR MAY JUN JUL AUG SEP OCT NOV DEC

1 2 3 4 5 6 7 8 9 10 11 12 13 14 15 16 17 18 19 20 21 22 23 24 25 26 27 28 29 30 31

JAN FEB MAR APR MAY JUN JUL AUG SEP OCT NOV DEC

1 2 3 4 5 6 7 8 9 10 11 12 13 14 15 16 17 18 19 20 21 22 23 24 25 26 27 28 29 30 31

JAN FEB MAR APR MAY JUN JUL AUG SEP OCT NOV DEC

1 2 3 4 5 6 7 8 9 10 11 12 13 14 15 16 17 18 19 20 21 22 23 24 25 26 27 28 29 30 31

JAN FEB MAR APR MAY JUN JUL AUG SEP OCT NOV DEC

1 2 3 4 5 6 7 8 9 10 11 12 13 14 15 16 17 18 19 20 21 22 23 24 25 26 27 28 29 30 31

LIVE THE LIFE

"You lack a foot to travel?
Then journey into yourself..."
—Mevlana Rumi

Settling in…

Have you developed any
new routines or rituals on your trip?

Draw a map of an area you've gotten to know.
Mark your own landmarks,
like a café where you had a great lunch.

How is your destination different
from what you had imagined?

Do the locals know you are just visiting?
What gives it away?

Write about something that made you
smile or laugh.

Have a travel companion or someone you met
leave you a note or a sketch.

Buy a postcard and send it to yourself back home.
Later you can add this to your journal.

JAN FEB MAR APR MAY JUN JUL AUG SEP OCT NOV DEC

1 2 3 4 5 6 7 8 9 10 11 12 13 14 15 16 17 18 19 20 21 22 23 24 25 26 27 28 29 30 31

JAN FEB MAR APR MAY JUN JUL AUG SEP OCT NOV DEC

1 2 3 4 5 6 7 8 9 10 11 12 13 14 15 16 17 18 19 20 21 22 23 24 25 26 27 28 29 30 31

"Though we travel the world over to find the beautiful,
we must carry it with us, or we find it not."
—Ralph Waldo Emerson

JAN FEB MAR APR MAY JUN JUL AUG SEP OCT NOV DEC

1 2 3 4 5 6 7 8 9 10 11 12 13 14 15 16 17 18 19 20 21 22 23 24 25 26 27 28 29 30 31

JAN FEB MAR APR MAY JUN JUL AUG SEP OCT NOV DEC

1 2 3 4 5 6 7 8 9 10 11 12 13 14 15 16 17 18 19 20 21 22 23 24 25 26 27 28 29 30 31

JAN FEB MAR APR MAY JUN JUL AUG SEP OCT NOV DEC

1 2 3 4 5 6 7 8 9 10 11 12 13 14 15 16 17 18 19 20 21 22 23 24 25 26 27 28 29 30 31

"Our battered suitcases were piled on the sidewalk again; we had longer ways to go. But no matter, the road is life."

—Jack Kerouac

JAN FEB MAR APR MAY JUN JUL AUG SEP OCT NOV DEC

1 2 3 4 5 6 7 8 9 10 11 12 13 14 15 16 17 18 19 20 21 22 23 24 25 26 27 28 29 30 31

JAN FEB MAR APR MAY JUN JUL AUG SEP OCT NOV DEC

1 2 3 4 5 6 7 8 9 10 11 12 13 14 15 16 17 18 19 20 21 22 23 24 25 26 27 28 29 30 31

JAN FEB MAR APR MAY JUN JUL AUG SEP OCT NOV DEC

1 2 3 4 5 6 7 8 9 10 11 12 13 14 15 16 17 18 19 20 21 22 23 24 25 26 27 28 29 30 31

"Adventure is worthwhile in itself."

—Amelia Earhart

JAN FEB MAR APR MAY JUN JUL AUG SEP OCT NOV DEC

1 2 3 4 5 6 7 8 9 10 11 12 13 14 15 16 17 18 19 20 21 22 23 24 25 26 27 28 29 30 31

JAN FEB MAR APR MAY JUN JUL AUG SEP OCT NOV DEC

1 2 3 4 5 6 7 8 9 10 11 12 13 14 15 16 17 18 19 20 21 22 23 24 25 26 27 28 29 30 31

JAN FEB MAR APR MAY JUN JUL AUG SEP OCT NOV DEC

1 2 3 4 5 6 7 8 9 10 11 12 13 14 15 16 17 18 19 20 21 22 23 24 25 26 27 28 29 30 31

JAN FEB MAR APR MAY JUN JUL AUG SEP OCT NOV DEC

1 2 3 4 5 6 7 8 9 10 11 12 13 14 15 16 17 18 19 20 21 22 23 24 25 26 27 28 29 30 31

ADVENTURE

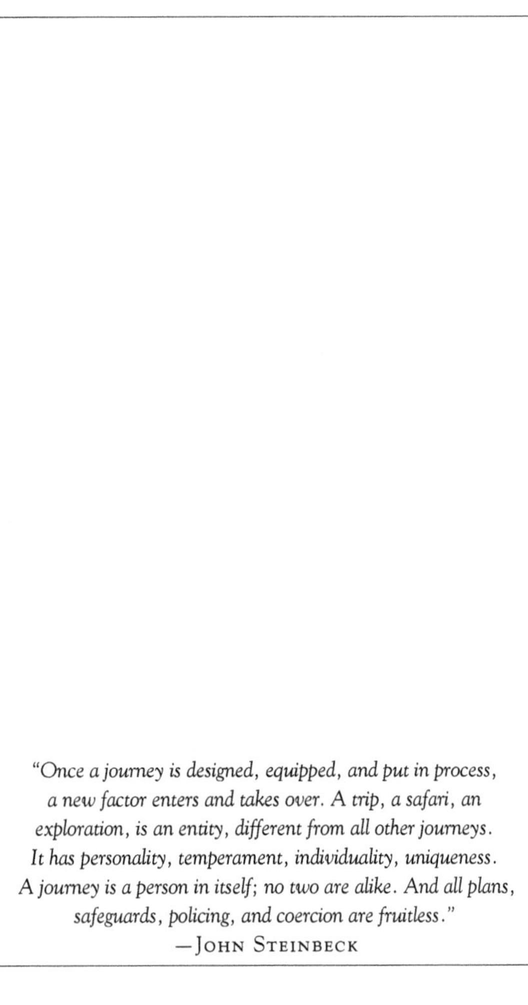

"Once a journey is designed, equipped, and put in process, a new factor enters and takes over. A trip, a safari, an exploration, is an entity, different from all other journeys. It has personality, temperament, individuality, uniqueness. A journey is a person in itself; no two are alike. And all plans, safeguards, policing, and coercion are fruitless."

—John Steinbeck

As you travel along…

Choose a different topic each day
to observe and think about.
It could be anything: food, clothes, children,
other tourists, language barriers, transportation.

Write about your three favorite meals
in this place so far.
Describe the restaurants, the food, the people,
and if you tried anything you've never had before.

Did you feel culture shock at any point?
What experiences or events led to this?
Did this event surprise you
or make you uncomfortable?
Why or how?

Record any memorable
or interesting quotes from today.

Write about something you did that
was daring or adventurous,
that you surprised yourself by conquering.

JAN FEB MAR APR MAY JUN JUL AUG SEP OCT NOV DEC

1 2 3 4 5 6 7 8 9 10 11 12 13 14 15 16 17 18 19 20 21 22 23 24 25 26 27 28 29 30 31

JAN FEB MAR APR MAY JUN JUL AUG SEP OCT NOV DEC

1 2 3 4 5 6 7 8 9 10 11 12 13 14 15 16 17 18 19 20 21 22 23 24 25 26 27 28 29 30 31

"We live in a wonderful world that is full of beauty, charm and adventure. There is no end to the adventures we can have if only we seek them with our eyes open."

—Jawaharlal Nehru

JAN FEB MAR APR MAY JUN JUL AUG SEP OCT NOV DEC

1 2 3 4 5 6 7 8 9 10 11 12 13 14 15 16 17 18 19 20 21 22 23 24 25 26 27 28 29 30 31

JAN FEB MAR APR MAY JUN JUL AUG SEP OCT NOV DEC

1 2 3 4 5 6 7 8 9 10 11 12 13 14 15 16 17 18 19 20 21 22 23 24 25 26 27 28 29 30 31

JAN FEB MAR APR MAY JUN JUL AUG SEP OCT NOV DEC

1 2 3 4 5 6 7 8 9 10 11 12 13 14 15 16 17 18 19 20 21 22 23 24 25 26 27 28 29 30 31

"Life is either a daring adventure or nothing."

—Helen Keller

JAN FEB MAR APR MAY JUN JUL AUG SEP OCT NOV DEC

1 2 3 4 5 6 7 8 9 10 11 12 13 14 15 16 17 18 19 20 21 22 23 24 25 26 27 28 29 30 31

JAN FEB MAR APR MAY JUN JUL AUG SEP OCT NOV DEC

1 2 3 4 5 6 7 8 9 10 11 12 13 14 15 16 17 18 19 20 21 22 23 24 25 26 27 28 29 30 31

JAN FEB MAR APR MAY JUN JUL AUG SEP OCT NOV DEC

1 2 3 4 5 6 7 8 9 10 11 12 13 14 15 16 17 18 19 20 21 22 23 24 25 26 27 28 29 30 31

"Why think about that when all the golden land's ahead of you and all kinds of unforeseen events wait lurking to surprise you and make you glad you're alive to see?"

—JACK KEROUAC

JAN FEB MAR APR MAY JUN JUL AUG SEP OCT NOV DEC

1 2 3 4 5 6 7 8 9 10 11 12 13 14 15 16 17 18 19 20 21 22 23 24 25 26 27 28 29 30 31

JAN FEB MAR APR MAY JUN JUL AUG SEP OCT NOV DEC

1 2 3 4 5 6 7 8 9 10 11 12 13 14 15 16 17 18 19 20 21 22 23 24 25 26 27 28 29 30 31

JAN FEB MAR APR MAY JUN JUL AUG SEP OCT NOV DEC

1 2 3 4 5 6 7 8 9 10 11 12 13 14 15 16 17 18 19 20 21 22 23 24 25 26 27 28 29 30 31

"It is good to have an end to journey toward;
but it is the journey that matters, in the end."
—Ursula K. Le Guin

JAN FEB MAR APR MAY JUN JUL AUG SEP OCT NOV DEC

1 2 3 4 5 6 7 8 9 10 11 12 13 14 15 16 17 18 19 20 21 22 23 24 25 26 27 28 29 30 31

JAN FEB MAR APR MAY JUN JUL AUG SEP OCT NOV DEC

1 2 3 4 5 6 7 8 9 10 11 12 13 14 15 16 17 18 19 20 21 22 23 24 25 26 27 28 29 30 31

JAN FEB MAR APR MAY JUN JUL AUG SEP OCT NOV DEC

1 2 3 4 5 6 7 8 9 10 11 12 13 14 15 16 17 18 19 20 21 22 23 24 25 26 27 28 29 30 31

JAN FEB MAR APR MAY JUN JUL AUG SEP OCT NOV DEC

1 2 3 4 5 6 7 8 9 10 11 12 13 14 15 16 17 18 19 20 21 22 23 24 25 26 27 28 29 30 31

LEARN

"People don't take trips . . . trips take people."
—John Steinbeck

Capturing the takeaways…

What was the best day or moment on this trip?

How did this trip change your understanding of this part of the world?

What did you learn about yourself on this trip?

What souvenirs did you buy?
Did you buy gifts for anyone at home?

If you visited this location again,
what else would you see or do?
What advice would you give to someone
traveling to this place?

How did this trip lead you
to think about your next adventure?

JAN FEB MAR APR MAY JUN JUL AUG SEP OCT NOV DEC

1 2 3 4 5 6 7 8 9 10 11 12 13 14 15 16 17 18 19 20 21 22 23 24 25 26 27 28 29 30 31

JAN FEB MAR APR MAY JUN JUL AUG SEP OCT NOV DEC

1 2 3 4 5 6 7 8 9 10 11 12 13 14 15 16 17 18 19 20 21 22 23 24 25 26 27 28 29 30 31

"A journey of a thousand miles must begin with a single step."

—Lao Tzu

JAN FEB MAR APR MAY JUN JUL AUG SEP OCT NOV DEC

1 2 3 4 5 6 7 8 9 10 11 12 13 14 15 16 17 18 19 20 21 22 23 24 25 26 27 28 29 30 31

JAN FEB MAR APR MAY JUN JUL AUG SEP OCT NOV DEC

1 2 3 4 5 6 7 8 9 10 11 12 13 14 15 16 17 18 19 20 21 22 23 24 25 26 27 28 29 30 31

JAN FEB MAR APR MAY JUN JUL AUG SEP OCT NOV DEC

1 2 3 4 5 6 7 8 9 10 11 12 13 14 15 16 17 18 19 20 21 22 23 24 25 26 27 28 29 30 31

"There is no foreign land; it is the traveler only that is foreign."
—Robert Louis Stevenson

JAN FEB MAR APR MAY JUN JUL AUG SEP OCT NOV DEC

1 2 3 4 5 6 7 8 9 10 11 12 13 14 15 16 17 18 19 20 21 22 23 24 25 26 27 28 29 30 31

JAN FEB MAR APR MAY JUN JUL AUG SEP OCT NOV DEC

1 2 3 4 5 6 7 8 9 10 11 12 13 14 15 16 17 18 19 20 21 22 23 24 25 26 27 28 29 30 31

JAN FEB MAR APR MAY JUN JUL AUG SEP OCT NOV DEC

1 2 3 4 5 6 7 8 9 10 11 12 13 14 15 16 17 18 19 20 21 22 23 24 25 26 27 28 29 30 31

"We travel, some of us forever, to seek other states, other lives, other souls."

—Anaïs Nin

JAN FEB MAR APR MAY JUN JUL AUG SEP OCT NOV DEC

1 2 3 4 5 6 7 8 9 10 11 12 13 14 15 16 17 18 19 20 21 22 23 24 25 26 27 28 29 30 31

JAN FEB MAR APR MAY JUN JUL AUG SEP OCT NOV DEC

1 2 3 4 5 6 7 8 9 10 11 12 13 14 15 16 17 18 19 20 21 22 23 24 25 26 27 28 29 30 31

JAN FEB MAR APR MAY JUN JUL AUG SEP OCT NOV DEC

1 2 3 4 5 6 7 8 9 10 11 12 13 14 15 16 17 18 19 20 21 22 23 24 25 26 27 28 29 30 31

"Live, travel, adventure, bless, and don't be sorry."
—Jack Kerouac

JAN FEB MAR APR MAY JUN JUL AUG SEP OCT NOV DEC

1 2 3 4 5 6 7 8 9 10 11 12 13 14 15 16 17 18 19 20 21 22 23 24 25 26 27 28 29 30 31

JAN FEB MAR APR MAY JUN JUL AUG SEP OCT NOV DEC

1 2 3 4 5 6 7 8 9 10 11 12 13 14 15 16 17 18 19 20 21 22 23 24 25 26 27 28 29 30 31

JAN FEB MAR APR MAY JUN JUL AUG SEP OCT NOV DEC

1 2 3 4 5 6 7 8 9 10 11 12 13 14 15 16 17 18 19 20 21 22 23 24 25 26 27 28 29 30 31

"It is not down in any map; true places never are."
—Herman Melville

ORGANIZE

FLIGHTS / TRAINS / BUSES / RENTAL CAR

[#, departure or pickup times, confirmation #]

ACCOMMODATIONS / HOTELS

EXCHANGE RATES

US DOLLARS	COUNTRY/CURRENCY

METRIC / US CONVERSION CHARTS

CELSIUS	FAHRENHEIT
-10	14
-5	23
0	32
5	41
10	50
15	59
20	68
25	77
30	86
35	95

SPEED	
1 mile per hour (mph)	= 1.609344 kilometers per hour
1 knot	≈ 1.150779448 miles per hour
1 kilometer per hour	≈ 0.62137119 mile per hour

LENGTH		
1 inch	=	2.54 centimeters (cm)
1 foot	=	0.3048 meter (m)
1 meter (m)	≈	3.280839895 feet
1 kilometer (km)	≈	0.62137119 mile
1 mile	=	1.609344 kilometers (km)
1 nautical mile	=	1.852 kilometers (km)

WEIGHT		
1 gram (g)	=	0.001 kilogram (kg)
1 ounce	=	28.34952312 grams (g)
1 pound (lb)	=	16 ounces
1 pound (lb)	=	0.45359237 kilogram (kg)
1 kilogram (kg)	≈	35.273962 ounces
1 kilogram (kg)	≈	2.20462262 pounds (lb)
1 metric ton	=	1000 kilograms (kg)

VOLUME		
1 US fluid ounce	≈	29.57353 milliliters (ml)
1 US cup	=	8 US fluid ounces
1 US pint	=	2 US cups
1 liter (l)	≈	33.8140227 US fluid ounces
1 US gallon	=	3.78541178 liters

ADDRESSES FOR POSTCARDS

Name

Address line 1

Address line 2

City, state, zip, country

Name

Address line 1

Address line 2

City, state, zip, country

Name

Address line 1

Address line 2

City, state, zip, country

ADDRESSES FOR POSTCARDS

Name

Address line 1

Address line 2

City, state, zip, country

Name

Address line 1

Address line 2

City, state, zip, country

Name

Address line 1

Address line 2

City, state, zip, country

TRAVEL TIPS

1. Familiarize yourself with your destination before you go—look at maps and read about various landmarks. It will all seem more familiar when you get there if you have a head start.

2. Wake up early and see popular sights before they are crowded with tourists. Bonus: You will take better photos with morning light.

3. Purchase travel insurance soon after booking your travel. Even though it can't replace your journal if it's lost, at least you can replace other more expensive items and be refunded money on last-minute travel cancellations along the way.

4. Break out of your comfort zone—try something new!

5. Travel on foot—you'll learn a city best this way.

6. Get lost on purpose—you'll be surprised at what you find! (But be sure to take along a map and your hotel information.)

7. Avoid long lines at popular attractions by making reservations in advance. Some can even be scheduled and paid for before you leave. Just remember to bring all confirmation numbers and printouts with you. Didn't plan ahead? Look for a less-crowded side entrance.

8. Stay hydrated, eat well, and get enough sleep!

9. Go where locals go—find off-the-beaten-path eateries and activities.

10. Connect with the concierge at your hotel. They are very knowledgeable and can give you some helpful tips. They can sometimes order tickets for shows or special exhibits at museums, so you avoid long lines at ticket counters.

11. Research public transportation and museum pass combos in the cities you are visiting. This can save a lot of time and money.

12. Check your rental car to see if it takes diesel fuel—making the mistake of putting the wrong fuel in your car can destroy an engine in an instant!

TIPS I LEARNED ON MY TRAVELS

PACKING TIPS

1. Don't forget your passport and a backup photo ID, such as a driver's license or state ID. Make photocopies of these documents, leaving one at home and bringing one with you.

2. Notify your bank and credit card companies you are traveling.

3. Bring more than one credit card and ATM card. That way, if one has a problem, you have a backup. Check if your bank partners with a bank where you are traveling—this may avoid ATM fees.

4. Be sure to share you itinerary with someone at home, so they know how to reach you if needed.

5. If you'll be crossing borders, check your cell phone plan before you go to be sure your phone will work in other countries. This can take time to set up, so plan ahead.

6. If you're bringing a computer, tablet, or smart phone, back up your devices before you leave. And don't forget your charging cords!

7. Bring an adapter and international plug converters for electronics. Most sold now also have USB ports.

8. Pack light. If you're questioning whether to bring something, you don't really need it. Try to fit everything into carry-on luggage if you're flying—but be sure to check the airlines fee policy for carry-ons to avoid being surprised at the airport!

9. Check all airport restrictions and guidelines. All liquids packed in your carry-on must be in containers no more than three ounces, and all combined have to fit in a one-quart ziplock bag.

PACKING LIST

POINT PAGE & VITAL WORDS

Symbol	Translation	Symbol	Translation

If this journal is found,
please be so kind to return it to:

Name

Address line 1

Address line 2

City, state, zip, country

Email address

Phone

Emergency contacts

Name

Email address

Phone

Name

Email address

Phone

www.ingramcontent.com/pod-product-compliance
Lightning Source LLC
LaVergne TN
LVHW052354100826
845147LV00013B/837

* 9 7 8 1 5 1 6 2 6 0 2 5 6 *